I don't need to dream

(True words poetry)
m. r. abdullah

*i don't need to dream because i am
(God-willing = insha-Allah) going to
jannah (paradise)...*

Your future my future
and those of us
who are alive at present on
earth at the moment
our future is fixed
depending on
what you or I believe in.

Let me explain
You see life is permanent
The real you is
your Soul (Ruh)
and the real me is my soul (Ruh)

The soul (Ruh) is real
because healthy people with
healthy organs die all the time
but they should not because
they have healthy organs,
this proves there is a soul inside us
and or something very sophisticated
and special (soul) created and
programmed by the Creator (Allah)
this soul keeps us alive until the
Creator reclaims it, when we face death
and the earthly body stops to function.

The real you is your Soul
not your earthly body.
Life is an examination,
earthly life is the examination
because of the free will.

The free will allows autonomy
therefore good and bad
Reward or punishment

You decide where
you end up
(providing your brain
and mind is functional)

The choice is yours.

reward (Jannah)
which is paradise
or punishment
which is Hell-fire,
(fire of jahannam)

**therefore your future
is in your hands.**

If you choose to live
a non-muslim life
and face death as
a non-muslim
then you will
face punishment.

If you choose to live
a muslim life
(islam=Quran and Sunnah)
and face death as a muslim
then the Creator
(Allah) will
reward you with
(jannah) paradise.

Having said all this
The Creator (Allah)
Knows best.

Why islam?

Islam is the truth
from the creator
but how and why?
the following facts
and more... makes islam
the truth

read the book
Devine Reality
by Hamza andreas
Tzortsis

Watch the youtube video
of Yusuf Estes, story of
yusuf estes, from
darkness to light

Also, How the bible
led me to islam,
Joshua evans.

A

The Quran since it has been
written down 1400 years ago
has not changed (114 surahs
then and 114 surahs now,
present day)

B

The Quran and Sunnah,
in other words deal with
free will, negative and
positive nature
and
especially islam
goes against
(Children of Adam)
mankinds' desires,
don't be arrogant ,
no sex before marriage,
no alcohol, no drugs
and so forth.

C

Islam, Quran and
Sunnah
explains
the wisdom behind
pain and suffering.
Every other religion
cannot answer
the question of
pain and suffering.
The creator (Allah)
says in the Quran.
That (Children of Adam)
mankind,
all of us will be
tested with health,
wealth, death
and so forth.

D

Islam, Quran tells
the muslims to
ponder over the
creator's creation
such as the planets
and the galaxies.
(the complex cell,
thousands of
different types of
species etc...)

E

islam, Quran says
everything will
perish and so does
the scientists that
the sun will become
a red giant and
swallow up the earth
and also the cosmos
(universe / multiverse)
will suffer a heat
death (lose all its
energy and die)

F

Islam points
out that
the life
we are living,
the earthly life,
it is a test,
the journey of life
is full of tests.
In which it answers the
pain and suffering.
Those good and true
muslims who
are patient will be
rewarded more
in the next life.
In the life to come,
Rewarded more

G

Islam, the Quran,
the creator mentions
sustenance,
maintenance and care

We all have systems
in our bodies
that we take for granted
such
as the circulatory system
and
the digestive system,
endocrine system
and so forth

The composition of
the gases
that is air, nitrogen,
oxygen
and argon,
all this is maintenance
and care
from the creator
Which proves
the creator has plans for us

H

The Quran
mentions
obedience
and
disobedience,
this is free will,
this is negative
nature
and
positive
nature
because
we have free will
therefore
we can, and do
disobey
or obey
the Creator (Allah).

I

Importantly, islam
has **Deterrents**
such as no Alcohol,
No Drugs, no Gambling.

These, **deterrents**
applied in
one's life does help
The child of Adam

(Try it out!)

J

Not to mention the
linguistic miracle
of the Quran
see yutube videos
for example,
nouman
ali khan – linguistic
miracle of the Quran
part 1 and 2

K

Also not to forget,(importantly)
Very importantly

that islam is from
the beginning from Adam
(peace be upon him)
the first man and prophet
and completed with
the final and the
last prophet, Muhammad
(peace be upon him).

L

Read the book
Devine Reality
by Hamza
Andreas Tzortzis

Read the Quran
Translation my
MAS Abdel Haleem
objectively

M

Read the book
signature in the cell
and darwin's doubt
by Stephen Meyer

N

**Read the Quran
(English) translation
by MAS Abdel Haleem**

(with an objective mind)

So if you experience
death as a muslim you
get rewarded with Paradise.

If you experience
death as a non-Muslim
then punishment.

Summary
Life is permanent
the earthly life is
the examination
(the real you is
your Ruh / Soul) after
experiencing death
paradise or Hell.

Yutube videos of Yusha Evans,

(How the bible led me to islam)

story of yusuf estes
from darkness to light.
Abdur raheem green and so forth

1

You see the difficult
test from The
Creator (Allah)
is the one of good
health and wealth
Life is permanent
the earthly part of
life is the examination

full of tests, big and small
from the Creator (Allah)

Don't forget, the real you
is your soul (Ruh)

subjective experiences in
one's life can lead
to misguidance
this is why it is important for
you and i to be
objective about islam
objective about the Quran.
And objective about the sunnah

(what is the message
in what has been said
and or what has happened)

context and historical context.
To be taken into account.

2

Speculation and guesses

How easily the devil
persuaded you
Satan and the
devil is the same
Why don't you listen
to your logic
Stop being arrogant
and ignorant
How easily the devil
persuaded you, to guess
to speculate.

The devil has put you
on a path to destruction.
Wake up, wake up before
it's too late.

Speculation and guesses
I thought
you had more sense than this.
You let your arrogance and
your ignorance dictate you.

Get logical get rational
You can still fix this.
Wake up to the logic
in your head.
Wake up to the logic
in your brain.
Wake up to the logic in your mind.

Freedom without structure
and without responsibility
is not freedom,
it is in fact individualism
in the extreme,
which encourages
prejudicism and racism

Don't forget, the real you
is your soul (Ruh) so the
wrong you do, is you do
to yourself.

Healthy people with
healthy organs
(young and old) shouldn't die?
They are healthy and
they have healthy organs
so they should not die
but they do.

So the question is what
keeps us alive?

the soul (Ruh) inside the earthly
body keeps us alive.

The real you is your soul (Ruh)
The soul is invisible.
The soul is intelligent, it provides
free will, autonomy
Soul and mind go together.
Earthly body and brain go together

**A child of Adam is not a child
of Adam without a Soul (Ruh)
The Creator (Allah) says in the
Quran; every soul (Ruh)
will taste death.**

Something in the future
which will look like us
and talk like us is just an advanced
machine without a soul which has
nothing to do with a
child of Adam's
reward or punishment.
It is not included in
the Creator's (Allah's)
autonomous
permanent life programme,
soul based. The real you
is your soul (Ruh)

An advanced synthetic earthly body
with a super (chip) computer inside
it, to simulate consciousness
is just an advanced machine
which looks like a child of Adam but it is not.

The biggest trick the Devil (satan)
pulled is to convince us that
he does not exist because then
he can influence you and
you won't know, influence you
towards your negative nature.

speaking the truth

Freedom of expression
should not be about
insulting other people
it should be for
speaking the truth

islam is the objective truth
why islam? Read the book:
Devine Reality by
Hamza Andreas
Ttzortsis and also
the Quran – English
translation by
M.A.S Abdel Haleem

The Creator (Allah)
has created everyone
(the children of Adam)
with a soul (Ruh) and the
real you is your soul
which is subjected to
reward or punishment

5

individualism

Dr Ken Hovind
(YouTube)
says:
Evolution is
a science disguised
in philosophy.

Read the book
signature in the cell and
DARWIN'S DOUBT
by Stephen meyer and
you will understand

**A child of Adam
is not a child
of Adam without
a Soul (Ruh)
The Creator (Allah)
says in the
Quran;
every soul (Ruh)
will taste death.**

Something in the future
which will look like us
and talk like us
 is just an advanced
machine without a
soul which has nothing
to do with a child of
Adam's reward or punishment.

(subjective) Twisted ideas

When you don't believe in
islam in (Allah = the creator)
When you don't believe in
islam the Quran and Sunnah
This is when you come
up with your twisted ideas
about God (Allah = the creator)
Such as the film,
x-men (apocalypse).

Having God complex issues
And questions
such as
why did God created me?
Did i ask God to create me?
this is to do with being arrogant
and ignorant and being
ungrateful to the one
who created you, and that is
t he Creator (Allah).

a rational person would
not be ungrateful
You wouldn't be ungrateful
to your employer.
You wouldn't like
your children to be
ungrateful to you.
You wouldn't like your
employees to be
ungrateful to you

So then why are you being
Ungrateful to, the
Creator (Allah) the one, who made you.

7

amazing paradise

awesome paradise,
(Jannah)
Paradise is amazing
More than amazing
No diseases,
no illnesses,
no viruses...

Worshipping
the creator (Allah)
is being grateful
to the creator
for the never ending
and amazing paradise
that you get to live in,
it will be awesome,

insha-Allah and
Alhamdulillah

8

Tests

just to make things clear
the life that we are living
right now is a test,
an examination,
full of big and small tests.

Right now on earth
we are being
tested by the
creator (Allah)
this is because we did
not create ourselves and
because we have been
given free will

and evolution is not true
read
signature in the cell
by Stephen meyer
Also
Darwins doubt
by Stephen meyer

Happiness Forever

Look,
it is straight forward
The creator created us
to test us
this is why we
have
negative nature
and positive nature

If you become a muslim
and die(experience death)
as a muslim then
you go to paradise
and live with the creator
in happiness forever
this is what i call
permanent success

Everything is free forever

my creator and
your creator
is the same creator
worship the
creator (Allah)
as a muslim
and so the
creator can
give us paradise
and free us
from our needs
No need to
work to eat,
no need to
work to have
a house with
a mortgage

In paradise
everything
is free forever
Permanent success
with
happiness forever

11

The judgement day

The Creator knows best
and the creator knows
when judgement day
will happen, when it
will take place
just after the world, has
come to an end.

so the creator can
reward you or punish you
depending on how you died
(experienced death)
as a good muslim
or a non-muslim

Importantly the key thing
to understand is this
The Creator created us
so the creator can
and want to give us
paradise but
some conditions have
to be met
according to the Quran.
(rules you have to follow)

words in the Quran are
from the Creator (Allah).

Islam is Quran and Sunnah
Islam is not a religion but
importantly the objective truth
From the Creator (Allah)

**Allah means the one who deserves
all worship.**

12

illogical

He chose arrogance
He chose ignorance
Why doesn't, he
be logical
who? Richard Dawkins

is he intelligent?
so he thinks
is he better than us?
So he thinks
that is just arrogance.

Is he going to live forever?
Is he not going to die?
(face death) experience
Death.

The real him is, his soul (Ruh)

we don't die, we experience death.

13

Obvious

We exist therefore
there is a creator
because we did not
create ourselves
This is obvious

this is not rocket
science,
a child will
understand
this,
I mean c'mon,
get real

(You unwise men
and women)

14

Read the books:

shattering the myths
of Darwinism
by Richard Milton

other books Darwin's
black box by Behe

and Signature in
the cell
by Stephen Meyer

and also
Evolution Deceit
by Harun Yahyah

these books will make
you think logically
and open your
eyes for real

"real talk"

15

Life is permanent

Death itself makes
life worthless
if you believe
there is no Creator.

But ask yourself
this (to an atheist)
how do we (human)
really function?

We have super computers
that can do
very big calculations
in seconds
but without any – type of
energy the super computer
will not work,
you have to switch it on

But with us, you see, we go to sleep
and we get up
Nobody has to
switch us on
or switch us off (until
death occurs)

The Creator (Allah)
knows what you do

use to love me

He use to love me
when
i was skinny and
attractive

But after the baby
it was hard
to maintain
my weight

He found a
skinny one
He found a
younger one
He found a
Look-alike model

He left me
He broke my heart

Present reality is selfish
Present reality is unjust

Too much subjective love
(self-love)
Not enough objective love
(loving others, caring for
Others)

Present reality is selfish

Present reality is selfish
but it is part of
the examination.

Trials and tribulations

How is it selfish?
For example
a woman wants
a handsome man

and a man wants
a beautiful women.
Where is the love in that?

Like and dislike is subjective
Someone you like
someone else may dislike

Like and dislike
is a personal opinion

Would you marry an ugly man?
Present reality is selfish
Present reality is most of the
Time selfish, because most of us
Are almost always subjective

18

The real you is
your Ruh (soul)

The real you is
your Ruh (soul)
the real me is my Ruh

My earthly body and
your earthly body
stops to function,

when The Creator (Allah)
reclaims my Ruh (soul)
and your Ruh (soul),

this is when we
experience death,

and our examination
ends.

Life is an examination.
Full of tests from the
Creator (Allah)

Soul (Ruh)

The soul inside the
Earthly body is invisible

(invisibility is real, such
As our thoughts, such as
The space infront of us
Such as radio waves, etc...)

The autonomous soul,
Soul is autonomous
Soul with free will
(Dual nature)

We have free will
Therefore,
autonomy
This is obvious.

**free will allows
the Soul to be
capable of being
good or bad this,
proves life is
an examination.**

20

Soul

As for the Ruh
(soul) is it real?

**Yes it is because
healthy people
with
healthy organs
Suddenly die
all the time**

but they shouldn't
but they do this proves
our earthly bodies
is just a shell
a uniform not the
real you or me.

positive and negative

The Ruh (soul
is programmed
with free will
(autonomy)
by the Creator (Allah)

The Free will allows
and enables
good and bad,
behaviour,
positive and negative,
thoughts and actions.

Therefore free will
and dual nature
proves, life is an
examination.

Restrain

When you can't
restrain
(control) your anger

When you can't
restrain
your jealousy

When you can't
restrain
your hatred

When you can't
restrain
your greed

Darkness spreads...
Darkness spreads...

23

Ignorance

Book of his,
THE GOD
DELUSION,
has troubled me, and
my friends and
I am sure those of you
who have heard about it
and read it feel
the same way
so much arrogance
and ignorance

even stupid would
be cleverer than him

i am talking about
Richard Dawkins

24

so much arrogance

The characteristics
Richard is showing
matches with the
Satan (The Devil),

as he goes on to say
I rather believe in
a flying teapot
and a flying
spegatti monster,

this may seem funny but
it is absolutely not funny
because what he is doing
he is ridiculing the divine,
he is ridiculing the master
and the creator of the cosmos
so much arrogance and ignorance.

Richard forgets once
he was nothing
once we were all nothing.

It is the Creator (Allah)
Who created us, and everything.

Dual nature

The very reason
he is doing this
is because, he can
and this is due to the
fact because
he has free will

There is
something else
called the
dual nature
and this is
negativity and
positivity
which, we all have.

26

negative energy

He chose ignorance
and arrogance

illogical thinking is not smart
it is unwise.

So what Richard is doing
he is exercising his
negative energy
into insulting
God and the believers

Not only through his
book the God Delusion
but also through social
media and with
his friends
such as Sam Harris,
Danial Dennet
and Christopher Hitchens
this is sad

Respect

What I
understand from
the teachings
of Islam
and from my
parents
that a person,
man,
women and
children,
nobody should
disrespect
somebody else

give respect to earn respect.

28

listen to this

However,
by the way
listen to this

Sam Harris and
Danial Dennet
they think
we don't have
free will?
What do you think?

How stupid they are?
Don't answer this
It is a rhetorical
question.

29

We have choices

The devil had and
has free will
that's why the devil
went against God
Everybody knows that,

The devil showed
defiance, the devil
did that
because he has
free will

Basically
we have
choices
therefore we have free will

Richard Dawkins is not
only naive
but also foolish, how?

P.E.E, Page 77
(The God Delusion)
Considering Zeus,
Thor, Apollo etc

there is a test to be God
and if you fail
that test then you are not God (Creator)

A, God has to be immaterial
B, God has to be timeless
C, God has to be space less
D, God has to be eternal
E, God has to be uncreated
(by definition)

the Creator (Allah) is uncreated
the uncaused first cause.
someone, a supernatural,
had to start the creation
and also, constant
maintenance and sustenance
is from the Creator (Allah)

Choose Guidance

You see the inventor
of a hoover like
mr dyson will not be
inside the hoover

The inventor of
Microsoft software
will not be inside
the software

Therefore the Creator
is outside the cosmos
(universe / multi-verse)

I thought Richard Dawkins
was clever
but I guess I was wrong

May the Creator (Allah)
guide people
like Dawkins to islam

If they want guidance
then the Creator (Allah)
will guide them.

Nonsense

By the way the
fossil record is
no evidence for
macro-evolution
All it is, is imprints of
creatures on old
rocks and old skulls
of apes. etc

and old bones
of men
and women
insects
animals etc...

He theorized
hypothetically
that the single cell
is just a blob of jelly,
160 years ago

You ask any
geneticist today,
micro-biologist
and
they will tell you
how extremely
complicated is
a single cell

read
signature in the cell
and
Darwin's doubt
both books
by Stephen meyer

34

A single cell
to come
into existence
from non living
things
is 1 in 10 to the
power of 340,000
Operationally
impossible
no matter how
much
time you give it
So **chance** does
not work.

I hope my atheists
friends understand
this

Please read the book
signature in the cell
And darwin's doubt
by Stephen meyer

35

Different flies
come from a fly
the common
ancestor is
a fly, not a worm.

is not facts

This illogical
EVOLUTION
NONSENSE
is a subjective-scientific,
perspective
based
ideology

a belief which comes from
Darwin's imagination

So called natural
selection is
without intelligence
And nothing is
Without intelligence
especially not us
Our brains are very advanced.

So the software
which is our mind
had to be programmed
by a supernatural,
super intelligent
and a uncreated being
and that is the Creator (Allah)

As for random mutation
that is nothing but creativity
because random mutation
will give you cancer
I say again random mutation
will give you cancer.

Cancer is caused by mutations
(changes) to the DNA within cells.

37

If you become a muslim
and die(experience death)
as a muslim
then you go to paradise
and live with the creator
in happiness forever
this is what i call
permanent success

38

A single cell
to come
into existence
from non living
things
is 1 in 10 to the
power of 340,000
Operationally
impossible
no matter how
much
time you give it

The soul (Ruh) is real
because healthy people with
healthy organs die all the time
but they should not because
they have healthy organs,
this proves there is a soul inside us
and or something very sophisticated
and special (soul) created and
programmed by the Creator (Allah)
this soul keeps us alive until the
Creator reclaims it, when we face death
and the earthly body stops to function.